Feral Domicile

Figures adapted from Gustave Doré's 'Ugolino e Gaddo' (Inf. XXXIII)

Boyd Warren Chubbs

BREAKWATER

BREAKWATER BOOKS LTD.
JESPERSON PUBLISHING   BREAKWATER DISTRIBUTORS

100 Water Street, St. John's, Newfoundland
www.breakwaterbooks.com

Library and Archives Canada Cataloguing in Publication

Chubbs, Boyd Warren, 1955-
Feral domicile / Boyd Warren Chubbs.

(Newfoundland poetry series)
Poems.
ISBN 978-1-55081-249-7

I. Title. II. Series.
PS8555.H8F47 2008& bsp;   C811'.54   C2008-904971-3
© 2008 Boyd Warren Chubbs

Visual images are drawn and adapted from the engravings of Gustave Doré (1832-83, French artist) done to illustrate Dante's *The Divine Comedy* (c. 1861).

The author gratefully acknowledges support from the Newfoundland and Labrador Arts Council.

All images drawn by the author

Design and layout by Monique Maynard

Printed in Day Roman

ALL RIGHTS RESERVED. No part of this publication may be reproduced, stored in a retrieval system or transmitted, in any form or by any means, without the prior written consent of the publisher or a licence from The Canadian Copyright Licensing Agency (Access Copyright). For an Access Copyright licence, visit www.accesscopyright.ca or call toll free to 1-800-893-5777.

We acknowledge the financial support of The Canada Council for the Arts for our publishing activities.

We acknowledge the support of the Department of Tourism, Culture and Recreation for our publishing activities.

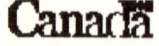

We acknowledge the financial support of the Government of Canada through the Book Publishing Industry Development Program (BPIDP) for our publishing activities.

Printed in Canada

Introduction

ON A NIGHT, A CLOSE NIGHT OF PRUSSIAN BLUE, A FIGURE leaves the house knowing when the lock clicks the only key is on the other side of the door, knowing there's no return. He roams the Old City speaking sonnets: some actual observations in real time; some upon memory. There's absolutely no evidence of a listener. He knows words emerge into failure, but he's compelled to continue, and the night passes into the other blue as he speaks his way into his new bed of earth.

1

From sleep at two or four
I found a way to life with a drink
from my friend, the brook by the door

and stared into the sweet chill
wondered who else dipped a cup
and long line of those who will

Through country where few have gone
communion climbed down and down
into broken geography; among

metals and mounds
and congregations melancholic, exultant,
shifting upon worried-bright grounds

The drink, the brook is seed—
a firmament lowering to need

2

I'm counting stars as they descend
where they starve and swallow
water. I'm lacing apricot gin

into my lips, numbed and longing
By old clocks, though broken
never stop, last of the waxing

moon drowns a black berry
Here, it's always day upon night
and night again for the weary,

the worried, the newly-wed
Seven stones fell from a friend's well
and the freed bucket swung into his empty bed

I'm wondering: to edit the Holy Book and it be read
what could be said or unsaid

3

By an outdoor table
I heard a palmist show a rich man
a path through the eye of a needle

All weather that day,
upon a wall that had seen everything,
was blasting away

blasting and hearing no one
But there, the teller of signs made
for her believer, a lund

a street-side grotto
a place where the hard wind
and its dosage couldn't go

The believer parted with a whistle on his lips
back to his span of cars, mansions and ships

4

Night is a summons, a summered-love
letting down velvet weather,
a deep-prussian glove

for the devoted. Wandering
unions around tables and albums,
in the tail-end of worlds, sing

by windows ajar
Creatures flattened by the day-stroke,
rise with the moth and star

and make a city in the feral air
A tender and deliberate tongue
makes, for the weary, a chair

But my door is nailed shut. Where can I begin?
This night has buried its keys in my limbs

5

The wanderer consumes wet-on-wet streets
Visible and apart
he lays nearest stars of the universe at the feet

of giver and taker; birds gone to bed;
faces starved for air
and, framed in uprooted prayer, by the head

of one beatified. Through a collection of beams
he reveals cobblers, coopers, scribes
devoted in cold dream

In the drenched-shimmering of this other world
owl and raven
bend churches and passed-by prophets; curl

vertical barrens and child's book. The tone
can't change, for the wanderer's always alone

6

The near face of clapboard and gable
and dogs quick to every shift and sound,
brought a feast to the traveller's table

He sent the return as mail–
weight and wonderment
soaked in ink upon a ghost sail

The old city was made
to enter his frame
in a surge through the soldier and slave

He went to the cathedrals, libraries and sea;
to the pub vineyards;
had hands on all the mason and carpentry

He went to the confessional, silent and bold
The listener's bench was vacant and cold

7

I went to a door to ask if God was there
A woman answered the knock
and said no, only people live here

To find God on earth
don't come to these apartments,
this steeple, this church

Down the street there's a man
who begs the day away
and sleeps when and where he can

speaking to no one, speaking to all,
through blizzard or sun-scorch
he keeps his place by the wall

Try there. Like the weather he's dark, he's bright
but always shines, without light

8

The Nazarene didn't travel far,
keeping his blood for the temple and lane
He didn't speak much, kept his tongue
for suppers, parables and the pain

of one who knew him best,
who kept her distance and mind
followed in a darkened dress
with ministry and wine

In a young year
he returned to the sound that made him move
speaking, I'm always with you
In the church of my small room

I'm raising a hymn, all of that and to you
saying wherever you are I am, too

9

Sun for this December day
is a liquid clementine,
a flowing sash
through the west window, upon the lying

ill where she's buried in thick quilt;
over red-birch floors onto lilac and jade;
lowering upon table, books and papers
and gifts travellers laid

It's all while the body's racked
with fever and chill
and what's passing and nearing
over Kenmount Hill

Each rub upon the face and bones advents
sabbaths and convents

10

I'm floating in water
The hand upon my head is strong
like chosen words from my late father

Before I'm submerged
one more look at the lichen and kelp
and birds

that rest here twice a year
One more thought for what I'm leaving
and I'm ready for the joy and fear

I found food, drink and company;
found an obscure, bright path,
epiphany in this country

Ready, now, to go under
and I'm plunged into the water thunder

11

Love comes on a summer's tongue
a glory-banner above
where I laugh and weep;
a story-manor where
child
and child sleep

It's a circling dream
like a feeding sparrow
or the immense, sculpted-gift of
the High Cross at Durrow

Everything I've received
came while I was still
like the new ghost, there,
upon my windowsill

12

Shine, shine, shine
said the sun to the moon
Turn to me the kind

side of your face and you'll live
above turbulent spring
and spare summers to give

lamplight where lovers seek private ground
and history is worn on the sleeve
There in the bay and town

prayers rise like winter-smoke;
triumph and despair blend,
tip and turn to soak

in some hybrid kerosene
Shine, shine and bless the strange dream

13

I kneel in capelin weather
with a rough, cold throat
I don't have my late-father's sweater

Makes ghosts of ghosts
this persistence
Sometimes hands are lost

and someone, lurching near,
seems to be a truck or blanket
Close, far or dear

is this gift on the long round-about,
slow weather toward invisible home,
the raw-speaking of love from the mouth

Tonight, there's no solution
Birth remains the revolution

14

Where a cast-iron lizard keeps the door ajar
love lies bleeding
A fatal weather pitched. Far

across the Cape
its tail flicks and wanders
I press a hand to the window and its speeding shape

It's not blood I find but hieroglyph,
a riddle, a ridged and rigid pattern
and no ladder to lift

me farther. The air is close
and light can't be named
They're no rescuing strangers on this coast

I'll miss love like the finest weather
that's passed forever

15

Green has gone to grey
Branches are severe, all knuckles and lance
ribs, knuckles and lance through this old, August day

I'm lost. No charts,
maps, schematics,
inukshuks or gifted hearts

to track the travelled year
and no bloodhound to know
the first tear

In the middle of night and tenderness,
without worry-stones or blanket,
I'm lost and stunned by the plummeting glass

If I'm found
it'll be by one who's in the ground

16

I'm speaking to the all-weather day just passed,
that many-headed and limbed bellow
I'm asking that it'll last

and return to these hilled-streets;
to the levels and dips;
upon all who venture and those who can't meet

Hard to see on this crisp day
the wind coming
to snap me away

Large keepers of buildings and grounds
hunt at leisure,
have perfect walls against these sounds

Light pushes in-and-out of favour
I remain, servant in devotion and labour

17

Death started full. By each dying, then
soon there'll be no death, death will have
finished all numbers it was given

I whistle this tune on the raw walk,
religion of step-upon-step
and the refrain remains in the talk

with the gull, crow and lichen
saying if it's true
it's true for everything

I whistle and believe
I do my poor dance
and falter where I give and receive

and sing if the last number is your breath
I'll rise and step to your life, your death

St. Patrick's bells
tour the glistened street,
roofs and soaked hills

October is filled with lead
dense with muted tongues
and a draped box of the dead

Rain drains into the bones
The procession turns beneath the steeple
as a slow-turning stone

But one leaned into the deadened lungs
and pushed a breath
showing mourners the ladder rungs

and said: Let him go as things have gone
Have heart. He'll reappear in song

19

I've heard of trade and trust
and caravans, this way,
bringing brightness and rust

and selling the used
as a way to give up your treasured
blinds as a freedom, not to lose

what you forged
but a liberation
between the new way and the Lord

The brightness is a too-bright war
I've seen the caravans
on the Island and Labrador

If there's trust
I'll place it in the rust

20

Hounds of winter call
through the brain
Through the memory wall

in their teeth, time as frozen light
shows bootmarks
where the few ventured that night

when weather dropped its gloves;
when March peeled oranges and
the Bay of Islands levitated
through all the stubborn rub

The hounds bring that long-ago bowl of rum
lifted to the winter-moon:
last sounds
from the last tongue

Don't turn the key too soon against day
Eager for the night garden
zeal can be a troubled way

to toss aside gifts;
communion of strangers;
fog on the bird cliffs

The mendicant hand, on a sober look,
is a cupped leaf,
a page from a holy book

The carnivals, in sleep,
can't conjure the geography
that drives the climber to keep

rendezvous with himself–
his clothes folded on the night shelf

Baggage and garbage lay
all around the moon
The lost and thrown-away

I see on this swift-clear night
praying I won't slip and die;
not lose sight

of promises the sea made
when it spoke upon the rocks
in tongues of jade

saying, you among the ruined and slain
will chase the genesis of dog-and-tale
while my patterns remain

All of this tonight I see
through the make-and-break memory

23

This day, bring yourself as gift
and your barrows and diggers
Bring vanes for windshift

For this day, my birth day,
bring your sadness,
that under-celebrated sobriety

These rooms split from need
Walls, floors split from those
who wouldn't, couldn't leave

Symmetry's gone
Across the one table we'll have to sing
my birth day song

You and the fair friends you'll bring
will restore walls and floors to their everything

24

Through this night a gull has the Tower in his mouth
I hear marbles loose down Victoria
and the judge of all talkers puts his shingle out

Lovers wait at the stop
saying, past the Cross there's no city
In the bucket-and-slop

of the politically-said
they're receipts and columns
that can't be read

Every now-and-then
I tap a glass I carry
to know when weather begins;

to know the soldier, mariner and aviator's head
or my father's, on his last and first bed

25

From a high-strung bow
pulled by a mighty arm
arrows shock into the high and low,

the raw regions where I'm naked and cold;
where the umbilical's coiled and gone;
the story told

I'm dragging myself toward a headland
Up a down rock case
I claw hand by hand

a spill of blood marking the way
Across the shore and other rough emptiness
arrows and bows have had their say

Panels and panels of dark and light drift home
I slump upon my birthday stone

26

There was no day, no night
when you reached to free him
I saw you give urgent care, marking each
book of light

when you beseeched divinity, old and new
there by your brother Lazarus
All the details blood made you

polished the plate and in copper graved
your blazing head when Christ came by
Weak and hopelessly-brave

I pray by this Herb Garden. My will is weak
but I pray for all of you, here
down deep-angled Springdale Street

Through flower and fountain, rock and rain
I breed and bleed your name

27

Love is the near and far
of measurement
It tells a book or star

their equal distance
from loneliness,
the spread between acceptance

and rejection; a hand-span that can't be said;
crucible for sea and land;
hieroglyph that can't be read

Love's a measurement brought
by a ghosted traveller to show
how close things are and are not

In my wondering corner; in my weak and strong,
when will my heart be ripped from the string it
                                                              lunges upon

What is this church I can't leave
Who is that priest
with gifts on his sleeve

of fire, land and water
that gave the last meal
to my father

This place that whips my head;
this tower of the chancel and pipes;
this book of the never-dead,

what is this view-master scene
with the height of colour and
torment of dream

Who's that inviting far down the aisle—
is that Mother or Child

29

I'm under a harvest moon
knee-deep in the bed of dogs
my head roaring with a tune

only the dead can sing
A lunar rainbow
bends over my praying,

over the hours of the Basilica
I remove my mouth,
my paralysed jaw

from the love that can't be said;
from words that cannot stand
and the book that can't be read

I hear the word of God
I'm speaking my listening into midnight sod

30

In your round-about,
in that impossibility
where you whisper and shout

will you lay claim to the main or shelf;
in your bravery
lay claim to yourself?

Names, names, names—
who would you call
without praise; without blame?

Sculpins become the new fish;
hills become mountains
and the water, grains in a fist

Who's at the sun's door
with or without a wish?

31

I heard a rainbow fall
fell as lovers must do
It sunk through the wall

of the Great Auk
and leaked onto headlands
where a poor traveller sought

roof and water
In the dark its colour bled;
its pot and gold stayed with the bird slaughter

The figure, without drink or shelter,
abandoned his clothes and paper;
folded his hands proper

Like myself, here, kneeling, crying
he went to sleep dying

It's the two of us now
A kind stray holds the moon in her jaws
Steamtrails from the heaven-ships somehow

have spread a cat's cradle across,
upon the prussian glove;
through the maples; around the cross

It's always the approaching hour
isn't it,
that one, the immaculate flower

unfolding in electric mystery,
time upon flesh
known, after love's history

It's the two of us now–
you and my vow

33

One breath and one thought
were gifted by a market
where nothing could be bought,

where there were no coins,
no engraved papers
and no trades that could find

what the eyes,
the heart,
the hands raking the skies

craved, in aching craved
and faltered 'til
they slumped upon the grave

The remains from that day, that night—
the absolutes of light

34

On your way make your own.
Dismiss nothing. Time, in its town,
will find you alone

and make a mark upon your head
where you kill the chair
or slump upon someone's bed

on your way to clear water–
to the come-home or stay-away year
where you call mother, father

The mirror gives another self
Draw that shape, that weather,
that shifting continental-shelf

Remember, rulers in or out-of-state
will be the same in casket weight

35

The finch is as massive as the eagle
In his own size he fills
the tree and sky, much as the beagle

is the height of the moose across barrens
or a grain of sand
is the width and breath of burial cairns

A fistful of light
can cover the rings of Saturn
and those rings equate with dark-bright

dimensions of galaxies beyond
Iron swelters in the forge–
the tongue and storms of the sun

A blade of grass started by a wind coming up
is a wilderness in my cup

36

What's time in a kiss:
the length of a table of suppers
where the young and never-young wish;

berries to berries pressed
beneath some strange weather
where there's no labour or rest;

a bell of prayers to ring and sing
and perfectly-enough to allow
nothing and everything;

a way to age, to rock
in the Labrador Sea
with the moon, without the clock?

What's time in a kiss–
what's a measurement that'll never exist

37

Gifts of gouda, raspberries and chard will
not bring light, nor gorgeous silk of words
bring warmth to the dark hill

All the weather–accordion of time,
fear and love–
wakes the roof off house, home and mind;

augers through wings of gulls;
makes mute those delicate and brittle;
drapes brilliant walls

Weather and book from the hill,
listing games for garments beneath love's broken head,
drain through an impossibly-mottled chlorophyll

It's nailed and nailed, here, west–
giver and thieves nailed in loneliness

38

Lovers and non-believers
have loved and non-believed since
wood was carried on the back

For lovers, the Second Coming was the Cross
but Science, the map and wax of its alphabet,
layered a floor over all of that

For non-believers it was all smoke and glass,
explosions and staggered light
No need for what lovers had made of the past

Cupboards are empty; cupboards are full
The glass drops for summer snow
Lovers and non-believers pull

out stored blankets and other clothes
and bury their heads in the remaining rose

After expansion–
all mass, length and time–
the universe will moor, finished tension

sighing to fetal sleep, the invention
giving back poems
writing, love is the fourth dimension

All's done and said
There's no space. The place is full
and it's the round of your head;

fathoms of your arms
in Da Vinci's *Vitruvian Man*
and the heart's alarm

The Carol of Carols will ring
without Listeners or Anything

40

She said: 'I am a moon. See
by other light
you'll find me'

I'm not holding a lamp
The wall to my back
isn't fire. It's a damp

burntwood where berries mysteriously return
I look. Ground and sky are black
Lights from a far car can burn

but not enough for a sweep of everything
She speaks and lures as from a distant wood
I turn and figure and then bring

from memory a sleeping ember to throw out
and it strikes upon the gleaming of her face and mouth

Three times on a Sunday, from an Arnold's Cove pulpit,
a sayer said true things
from an Eve of words he could commit

to after a long see-saw. We conjured salt,
sea, berries, dreams and levity
while a wind tore malt

from the glass and pillows. We agreed
sometimes there's a sign to tell how
a celebrated flower blew through a reluctant seed

The moon has stalled above this field
On this advent
sun pours morning-full. The moon won't yield
The moon has stalled above this field
The flower-of-morning is full. The moon won't yield

42

A sparrow's world is my world
much as yours might be a house of glass
where you work and build; or a curl

of metal the rat's tested in
is a home while the results
are tallied and reports begin;

or those catapulted to live among dust and stars,
in that colder, bolder place,
have windows to study wars

I'm climbing the ladder to my room,
spider and horse with me
I'm climbing into my working tomb

speaking to the connection of everything;
following loops of the impossible string

43

What's that last wave,
that left and right twist of the hand?
Is it goodbye or hello
to the dark; the light? Can

a figure know if the Sun God
destroys the weather clouds or they reappear
beyond the blink, bringing deserts
a rain for the year?

The Northern Flicker by windows,
with its brilliant slash of red,
is it lifting with a throat of seed
or past the house, fallen dead?

When you bring news on your return
bring me a question. So I learn

44

Its prism ensures I'm never a stranger;
gives levitation
Barrens melt danger;

smashes glass in my head
and locks my knees
Its grey, purple, black rocks stop me dead

Barrens live a touch above the ground
Berries and winter know
barrens have a sound

They're continuous, feral domicile–
bed for first love;
canvas for the child

They're gifts of tapestry Ancients wove
from Western Point to Grates Cove

45

Which is nearer, the heightened pub
or coarse arms of sleep,
poor dreams where they rub

raw, night toward day?
I could enter the fine drug
of bright eyes and stray

good words from wine and rum
or curl by this brick wall
where a fitful dark is a broken drum

and I know roaming dogs would give
their beating chests
as pillows for my head

Both impossibilities I've seen
I reach and find a coin for the answering machine

46

There's a catapult in the imagination
filled with multiplying bread for the child
The world's always tensed against that advancing nation,

that force, tongue and hand
loosed from a tilted stage
all its spread shape reaching crown land

erupting like the knifed cod's blood
and no wall can turn its road;
no wall has withstood

those illuminated collisions
among raven, pigeon, sparrow, gull
Lurking mysteries become overt in the colliding visions

It's the many-headed puzzle a switch gave
to mourners trudging to the grave

Something stirred from what a stranger said
In a close dark it stirred a sober sight–
a Eucharist table in his head

After the feast, mint from a fresh-cut tree
lay upon his bare garments
and merged with elixirs from the salt-sea

He stumbled into a room of gifts
and towering models to follow
but shoved back to drift

again, among lanes and stones;
read ashes emptied from stoves;
read full-blooded notes thrown

to the dirt from forbidden love
He drank his night from a prussian glove

48

At death my library will be complete
My body, having nothing to donate,
will root, scholastic and replete

Water will wash feet of the gull and its head,
will bend to let boats in;
lift sparkled Alps to Gibralter and sailor's bed

Winter will have its beard and folds
Lovers'll stain rocks again with
first love, young and old

Summer, bronzed swimmer, will
reach long into October's
basket and quill

I'll be lying in marked pages
finished with wages

49

Midnight's receiving light
Torches from the Yard
yield to their beds. A slight

cough of wind steers paper scraps
down Job Street;
finds pigeons and men-in-caps

pronouncing the hours away
From this earthen floor
I lift my boiling head

and my broken side
My house is distant forever
and the water's turbulent and wide

I see a dog finding the final bone
and now the sun mating with the moon

50

Night restored him full
He grinned from his grave at Plank Road
counting torches from his buried window

seeing welders fire cold steel onto a ship's head;
fire lunging upon that field;
healing fire in the St. John's ship-bed

Shadow by fire, light by fire
he lived in exile
by devotion and desire

Above, vultures and gods wore
themselves to kiss, scouring the place
to find lightning he gave the rich and poor

There, in his box of earth, he knew life was loaned
but fire is fire and can't be owned

www.ingramcontent.com/pod-product-compliance
Lightning Source LLC
Chambersburg PA
CBHW032136090426
42743CB00007B/610